Master Clas[s]

Magic

Written by Maurice Day
Illustrated by Pete Moore

HENDERSON
PUBLISHING PLC

So... you want to be a magician?
This book will show you how. Many professional magicians started by reading books like this one. I did. Perhaps you will too!

YOUR EQUIPMENT

No self-respecting Magician would begin their routine without a wand. You can make your own very cheaply:

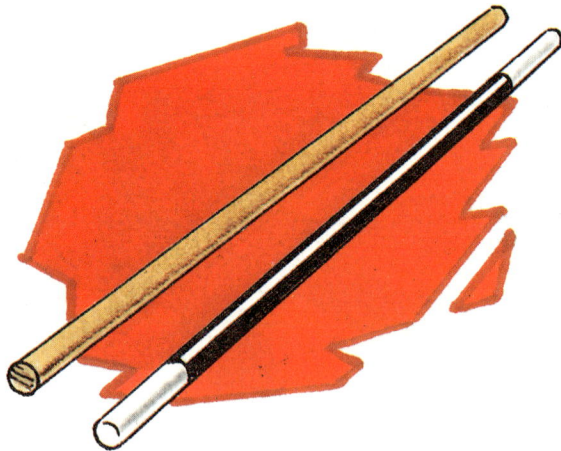

Easy Wand 1

Buy some dowelling 30cm long. Paint it white at either end (each tip about 4cm long) and black in the middle.

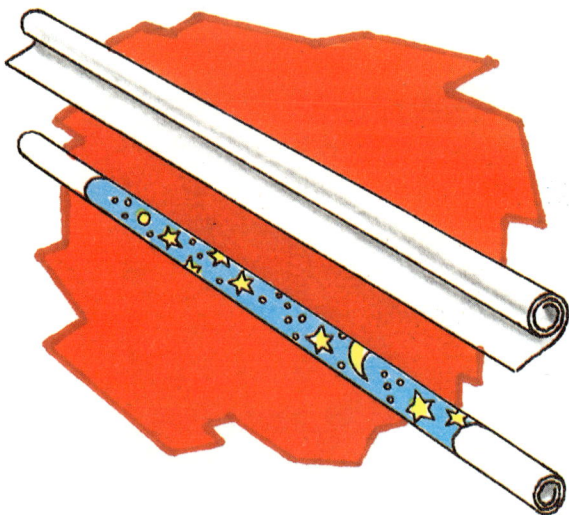

Easy Wand 2

Paint a thin card tube (make one with stiff paper) black. Paint the tips white, as above. Decorate with metallic stars or glitter.

When you perform your magic, it's a good idea to have a small table to put your props on. A card table or fold-away table would be ideal.

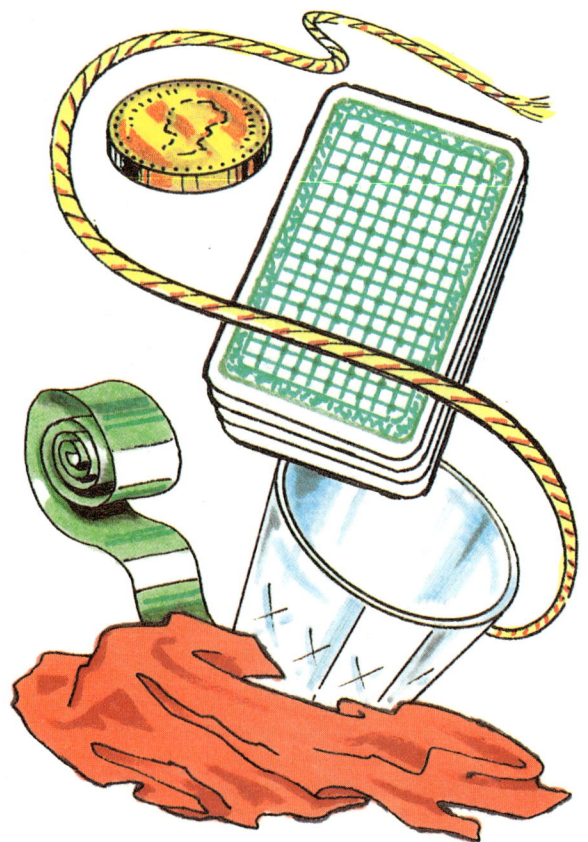

For the tricks themselves, you'll be using ordinary objects such as coins, string and, of course, playing cards. Some tricks will require simple materials like card, paper and scraps of cloth.

Practise, Practise, Practise

Once you've created your trick, you'll be itching to show it to your friends. STOP RIGHT THERE ..... the first, and probably the most important rule of magic is 'practise, practise and practise some more'. Then, and only then, can you show your new talents off!

Try every trick several times in front of a mirror. When you think you can perform it well, show it to Mum or Dad. They tend to be your kindest critics and can suggest any improvements you should make. Finally, you can show your routine to relatives and friends.

Your Patter

Decide whether you wish to accompany your tricks with amusing patter or perform in dramatic silence.

A shy, quiet person may be happier with a silent act. If you perform in this way, play some suitable, 'atmosphere building' background music from a tape recorder.

If you are feeling confident, present your tricks with lively chat. To help you, suggestions for your 'banter' are given with each trick in this book.

Your Costume

What should you wear? Whatever you choose, you should look neat and clean (scrub those nails - your hands will be in the spotlight!). Magicians wear anything from a top hat and cloak to a clown's outfit. How about a Merlin outfit? Simply decorate a conical hat with stars, moons and planets.

Your Routine

Open your show with a trick that is easy to do. This will give you confidence. Finish with your best trick.
Alternate tricks with short effects with those that take slightly longer.

Vary the type of prop used. A routine with five card tricks and one rope trick could be boring.

Use magic words and spells to enhance your tricks - 'Abracadabra' is well known. You could chant 'Hey diddle diddle, one two three ... magic spell, please work for me'!

3

How long should the act be?

Fifteen to twenty minutes is long enough. Select your tricks to give a variety of effects: production, vanish, transposition, mind reading and so on. Examples of all these types of tricks are given later on in this book.

Your stage fright!

Most professional performers are nervous just before the start of their act. They have various ways to calm their nerves. Some suck a boiled sweet. Others take several deep breaths. Another might do simple exercises to loosen tight muscles.

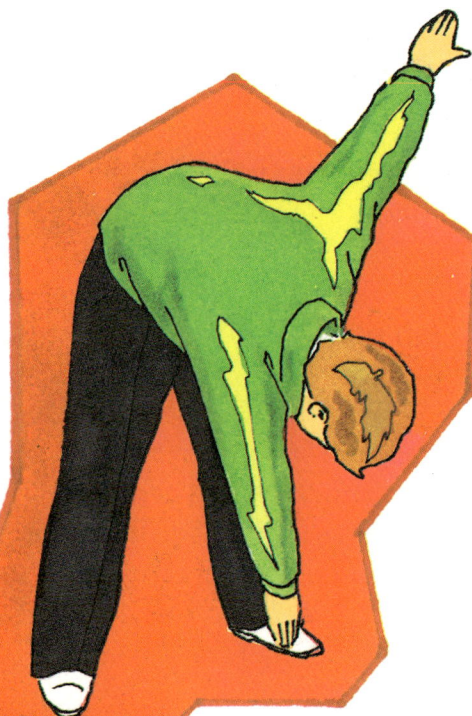

Don't be in a hurry to launch into your first trick. Introduce yourself. Look at all the faces in your audience. Give them a big smile. If you look as though you are going to enjoy yourself, they will relax and enjoy themselves too.

Your audience

Some tricks require an assistant from your audience. Avoid selecting a 'smart Alec'. They will try to spoil your act. Look for someone with a friendly smile who appears to be enjoying your magic.

At the end of your show, thank everyone for watching. Their applause will be music to your ears! You'll be hooked on magic and will look forward to the thrill of your next performance. Don't limit yourself to family and friends - offer your services at birthday parties and school functions.

Later on you may wish to meet other magicians to swap ideas. Check your area for magic clubs.

Contact another magician advertising in Yellow Pages or your local paper - they can help you find a suitable club.

AMAZING DETECTORS

Two metal rods swing across one another when held above a coin. Over water, they swing outward.

You'll need:

2 wire coat hangers

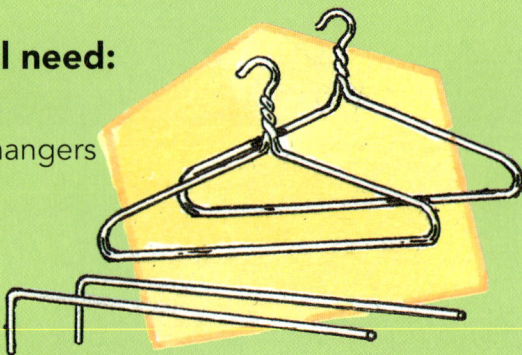

a glass of water

a coin

Preparation

Ask an adult to cut off the hook parts of the coat hanger wires. Straighten the remaining parts and make 'handles' by bending the ends down at right angles.

The Trick

1 Place the glass of water on the floor. Ask someone to hold your detectors loosely in each fist. The long parts extend in front of them.

2 Inform them that the detectors will swing outwards when held over water. To their surprise, it works.

3 Place the coin on the floor. Explain that the detectors will cross over one another when held over the coin... it works again!

How does it work? Automatically. If someone believes the detectors will move, their muscles make slight involuntary movements to make it happen.

Magician's Helper

If they don't work, give them to someone else. Sometimes a sceptical person fails to produce any result.

SOMETHING FOR NOTHING

A box is shown to be empty. Silky squares and a doll are 'magically' produced from it.

You'll need:

1 cardboard box some silky squares (can be bought from ethnic craft shops)

1 small doll (Batman, Action Man, Barbie, Thunderbird character etc.)

Preparation

Cut out an opening from one side of the box and discard it. Paint the inside matt black. Cut a panel of card to fit at an angle inside the box. It doesn't need to be fixed. paint this matt black both sides.

The Trick

1 Place your doll behind the flap, followed by the silky squares.

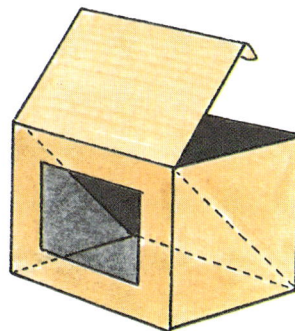

2 Tell your audience that you have a magic box. It appears to be empty.

3 Open the lid and let it hang down over the opening.

4 Say a magic spell and produce the silky squares. 'Batman bought these for his girlfriend', you say, 'Would you like to see him?'. Now produce the doll.

Magician's Helper

Never tell your audience 'This is an empty box' - they won't believe you! Simply say it is a magic box. Decorate the box with brightly-coloured fabric or paints.

MAGIC SPELL

Two spectators mix a pack of cards. You spell the name of each card from ace to king. As the last letter of each card is spelt that card is shown.

You'll need:

a pack of cards

Preparation

Arrange thirteen cards of different suits in the following order: 3, 8, 7, ace, queen, 6, 4, 2, jack, king, 10, 9, 5. The five is on top and all the cards face up. Place this set of cards behind a prop on your table so nobody can see them.

The Trick

1 Divide the rest of the pack of cards in two. Give one pile to someone to mix. Then give the second pile to another person.

2 When one helper has finished, take their cards and put them face up on the secret pile on your table. DO the same with the other helper's cards.

3 Bring the complete pack from your table and hold them face down. The arranged set are on top. Remove them (there will be thirteen cards) and discard the rest.

4 'These cards are good at spelling,' you say, 'Let me show you.' Spell the cards in order from ace to king. As you spell each letter transfer a card from the top to the bottom of your pack. The next card after the final letter each time is shown and discarded.
For example, when you spell ACE, three cards are transferred to the bottom of your pack and the fourth card shown and discarded.

Magician's Helper
Ask your audience to spell the cards with you. It makes the trick more interesting to them.

LINKING PAPER CLIPS

Several separate paper clips are dropped into a paper bag. The bag is blown up and burst. All the paperclips are now linked in a chain.

You'll need:
2 paper bags

50 paper clips
glue

Preparation
Cut one third from the top of the paper bag and discard it. Make a few holes around the centre of the bag. Link 25 paperclips in a chain and put them in the larger bag. Insert the smaller bag into the larger one and glue them together at the top.

The Trick

1 Drop the loose paperclips into the double bag.

2 Screw up the top and blow it up. The holes allow air to inflate the outer bag.

3 Burst it to display the chain of paper clips.

Magician's Helper
Ask someone to cup their hands under the bag just before you burst it. As they catch the chain, you screw up the bag and pop it into a waste bin.

RISING MATCHBOX

This baffling trick is excellent when you want to use matchsticks in your act.

You'll need:

a box of safety matches

a split pin or paper clip
sticky tape

Preparation

Ask an adult to cut a narrow slot in the matchbox cover with a craft knife. Slide the drawer into its cover. Push a split pin through one end of the slot and into the drawer. Slide the drawer out as far as it will go and bend both arms of the split pin. Fix them with sticky tape. If you can't obtain a split pin, use a paper clip. Bend it to shape. Push it through from the drawer so part X extends through the cover. Put some matches in the box and close it.

The Trick

1 Hold the box vertically.

2 Push up the head of the split pin with your forefinger.

Magician's Helper

To cover the action, make a few mystical passes over the matchbox with your free hand.

11

CLEVER FIREMAN

Telling a tale of a clever fireman you tear a roll of paper. Pulling up the centre part you produce a paper ladder.

Preparation

Glue together several pages of your newspaper by their edges. When the glue dries, roll up the paper from one short end (not too tightly). Glue the other short end to the roll.

The Trick

1 Flatten the roll. Tear out and discard a rectangular shape from one long edge.

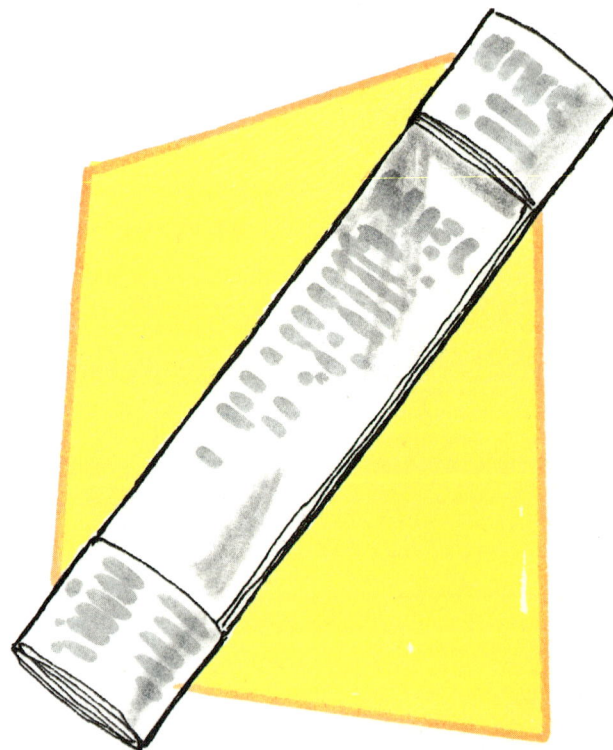

2 Open the paper into a roll again and flatten both folded edges together.

3 Bend down both outer rolls. Put your fingers inside these rolls and pull upwards.

4 Tell the story of a fireman who was on holiday. 'He spotted a fire in a hotel and someone was trapped on the top floor. He rolled up a newspaper, tore a piece out and made a ladder so that he could rescue the trapped person. Wasn't he clever?'

Magician's Helper
The more paper you use, the higher your ladder will be. Test a duplicate roll first - the roll must not be too thick for you to be able to tear it!

POACHERS AND FISH

This puzzling little trick works automatically. Matchsticks apparently jump from one hand to the other.

You'll need:
7 safety matches

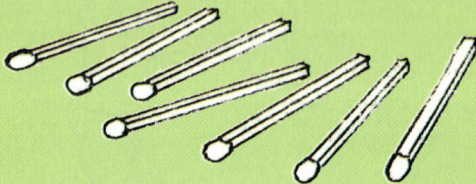

Preparation
Place five matches on the table, well separated. They represent salmon. Two matches, one in each of your hands, represent poachers.

1 Tell your audience 'Two poachers caught five salmon and decided to share them'. Pick up a match alternately in each hand, STARTING WITH YOUR RIGHT HAND.

2 You now have four matches in your right hand and three in your left hand. Don't let anyone see the matches in your hand.

3 Continue: 'The poachers were going off to sell their catch when they spied a warden in the distance. So they decided to hide the fish under a bush'.

4 Place the matches on the table one at a time, alternately from each hand STARTING WITH YOUR LEFT HAND. The fifth match (from your left hand) is actually a poacher so keep your hand closed as though it contained something.

5 You go on: 'When the warden went away, they shared out the salmon again'. Pick up the matchsticks as before, STARTING WITH YOUR RIGHT HAND.

6 'The strange thing was that one poacher took home four salmon and the other man took only one.' Open your hands to display the matchsticks - five in your right hand, two in your left hand.

Magician's Helper
Although it works automatically you must remember which hand to use at each phase of the trick. Practise it well.

MIRACULOUS MEMORY

A member of your audience is given a folded newspaper. They cut a small portion with scissors so they have a dozen or so small pieces of paper. Turning your head away, you hold the papers and ask them to take one saying, 'Don't let me see it'. Going into a corner of the room, you describe both sides of the paper they hold.

You'll need:

2 newspapers exactly the same

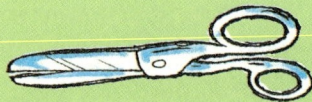

a pair of scissors

Preparation

Place pairs of pages together - two of page 1, two of page of 2 etc. Each page is duplicated. Use half the number of pages from each paper or it will appear to be too thick and arouse suspicion.

The Trick

When your helper cuts out a small section, you will have a set of duplicated clippings. When they remove one, you go to a corner of the room and look for the only single clipping. All you have to do is read it and describe any picture fragments.

Magician's Helper

Pretend to have difficulty when reading the contents of your slip of paper. Then it appears you are reading someone's mind - not merely performing a trick.

I'LL READ YOUR MIND

Four pieces of coloured paper are on the table. Someone is asked to choose one, mentally. As you tap each colour with your magic wand, your helper mentally spells out their chosen colour - one letter for each tap. They say STOP when you have completed as many taps as there are letters in their chosen colour. To their surprise, you have stopped on their selected colour.

The Trick

You'll need:

4 pieces of paper
(1 blue, 1 yellow, 1 red, 1 green)

your magic wand

Preparation
Place the papers far apart on your table.

Your first two taps are on <u>any</u> colour. All the succeeding taps are in the following order until you are stopped: 3rd tap on red, 4th tap on blue, 5th tap on green and 6th tap on yellow. You can't go wrong! Each colour has the same number of letters as the number of taps.

Magician's Helper
You can adapt this trick using cards with people's names on. Use any group of names - With 3,4,5 and 6 letters in.

SURPRISING SAUSAGES

Two sausages are shown. One appears shorter than the other. They are alternately stretched - one becoming longer than the other. Finally they appear to be the same size.

You'll need:

2 pieces of card

scissors

felt-tips or paints

Preparation

Cut the card into two curved shapes, each the same size. Draw a sausage on each one.

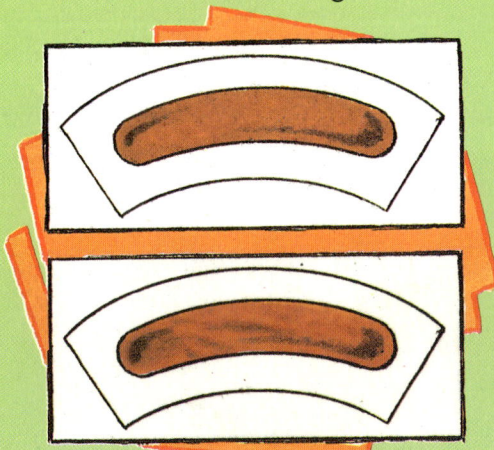

The Trick

1 Show the sausages one under the other. The top one appears shorter.

2 Pretend to stretch the top one. Place it <u>underneath</u> the other sausage. It looks longer. Repeat this.

3 Place them so the inner curves are together. The sausages now appear the same length.

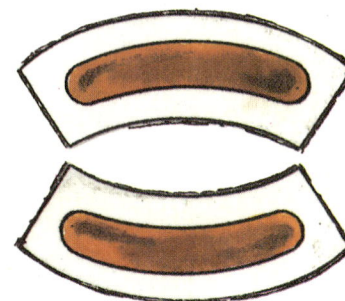

Magician's Helper

Make a big thing of stretching the sausages. Then your audience won't realise that it's an optical illusion.

Tell your audience the story of two children who each had a sausage for school lunch. One was upset because his was smaller. So he stretched it. Then the other child got jealous so she stretched her sausage. Their teacher settled the argument when she made the sausages the same size.

COPY CAT WAND

It's a good idea to inject comedy into your show. This trick does that and surprises your helper!

You'll need:

plastic tubing (from an electrical suppliers or builders merchant. It's called conduit piping. You need a piece 30cm long with an inside diameter of 1.5cm)
dowelling (cheap from a D.I.Y shop. It should fit easily in the tubing)

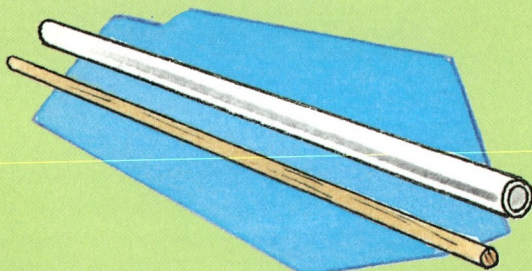

Preparation

Block one end of the tube with a disc of thick card or hardboard and glue in place. Cut your dowelling so it extends 2cm from the tube when placed inside it. Paint both 'wands' the same.

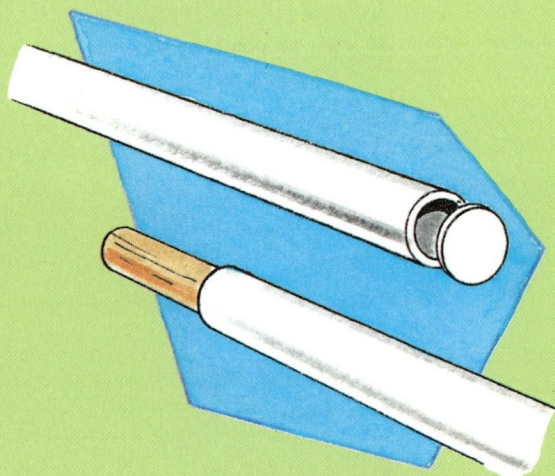

The Trick

1 With your wands nested together, hold them at the open end. Ask someone to hold the wand.

2 As they grasp it, grip the inner wand and move quickly away from your helper, sliding the wand out.

3 Look at your wand. Act puzzled. Look back at your assistant saying, 'Please take the wand .. oh, you did... it's copied itself!'

Magician's Helper

You could make the outer wand from thick paper. Roll it around the dowelling and glue it. Paper can be painted with gloss paint.

GENIE IN THE BOTTLE

A piece of string is lowered into a bottle. When the string is raised, the bottle comes with it.

You'll need:

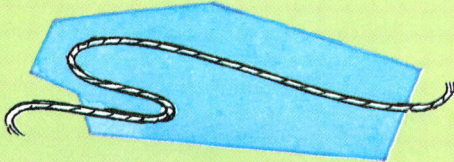

a piece of string about 30cm long

a piece of cork

a bottle with a narrow neck (bottle can be plastic, but must be opaque)

Preparation

Ask an adult to cut the cork into a small ball that easily goes into the bottle. Pop it in before you show the trick.

The Trick

1 Lower your string into the bottle.

2 Turn the bottle upside down. This causes the cork to wedge itself between the string and bottle neck.

3 Give a little tug on the string to jam the ball. Turn your bottle the right way up and let it dangle. To release the string, push it down a little into the bottle. The cork drops away and frees the string.

Magician's Helper

To avoid suspicion when you turn the bottle upside-down, you need an excuse. Tell your audience that you found the bottle and that a genie lives inside it. When you turn the bottle upside-down, peer into the neck and say 'Genie, could you hang onto the string?' When the string is jammed, you can swing the bottle from side to side. Ask the genie to let go of the string when you release it.

TOPSY-TURVY MONEY

A banknote is the correct way up. It is folded. When unfolded, it is upside down.

You'll need:
a banknote

The Trick

1 Place the note the correct way up and mention this fact. Fold it in half lengthwise from bottom to top.

2 Fold the right-hand half back to the left.

3 Fold it again so the left-hand side is folded to the right.

4 Now you unfold it. The top half is unfolded to the left.

5 The new top half is unfolded to the right.

6 Finally, unfold the top half downwards.

Magician's Helper
This trick can be done with any banknote, of course. If you're broke, simply cut a rectangle from a newspaper or magazine - it works just the same!

HEADACHE CURE

You show the spectators a picture of a boy with a headache. It is slid into a folded piece of paper. On opening the paper, the drawing has disappeared!

You'll need:

some thin, opaque paper
a piece of thin card
a felt tip pen
glue

Preparation

Cut the thin paper into two equal squares. Fold them in half both ways. Stick them together by gluing squares A, B, and C and the edge of square D. Square D forms a pocket with an opening at the top. Draw a picture of a miserable looking lad. It should be on a piece of thin card that fits easily into the secret pocket. Fold up B and C. Then fold C and D to the left. The pocket now faces you and you are ready to perform the trick.

The Trick

1 Showing the drawing you explain, 'This is Timmy Turtle. He has watched so many videos that he has got a bad headache. This paper cures headaches.'

2 Slip the drawing into the pocket. Wiggle your fingers over the paper. Unfold it and show both sides. 'Not only does it make the headache go away, it makes Timmy vanish as well!' you exclaim.

NOW YOU SEE IT, NOW YOU DON'T

You place a handkerchief on the table. A pencil is placed in the centre of the handkerchief. You fold the handkerchief in half. Placing both hands over the pencil, you roll the handkerchief away from you to form a cylinder. When you unroll it, the pencil should be <u>outside</u> the handkerchief.

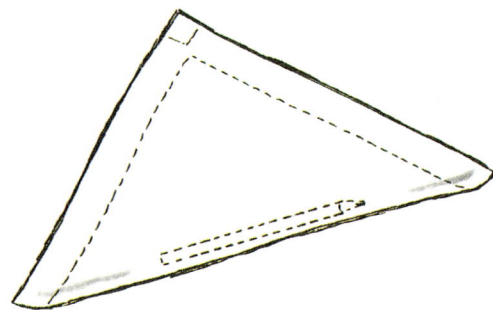

You'll need:

a pencil

a handkerchief

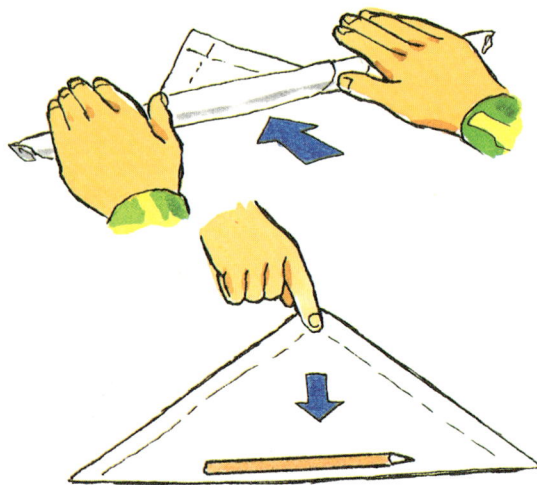

The Trick

1 Fold your handkerchief so that top corner A extends two or three centimetres beyond lower corner B.

2 When you reach the corners as you roll the handkerchief, let corner B go once over your pencil. Ask someone to hold the two corners against the table whilst you unroll the handkerchief back towards you.

Magician's Helper

You can reverse the process if you wish. Roll up the handkerchief around the pencil again until the corner that was underneath (A) goes over the top of it.
Unroll as before.
Don't repeat this trick more than twice - an eagle eye could spot the method.

X-RAY EYES

You show the spectators several different coloured crayons and a box. Whilst you are out of the room, someone chooses a crayon and puts it into the box. The other crayons are hidden.

On your return to the room, someone gives you the box behind your back. You announce the colour.

You'll need:

Crayons

A box

The Trick

Once the box is behind your back, open it and scratch the crayon with your fingernail.

Close the box. Keeping it behind your back, bring your hand to your forehead as though trying to get inspiration. As you do this, glance at your fingernail to detect the colour of the crayon.

Magician's Helper

You can do this trick with coloured chalks. In this case you don't scratch the chalk - simply rub your fingertip on it.

You can repeat the trick asking different folk to choose a crayon (or chalk). When you leave the room, you have plenty of time to remove the previous colour from your finger.

MAGIC BALLOON

A balloon is placed into a carrier bag. It is burst with a pin. On removing it from the bag, it is not only whole again, but it has also changed colour!

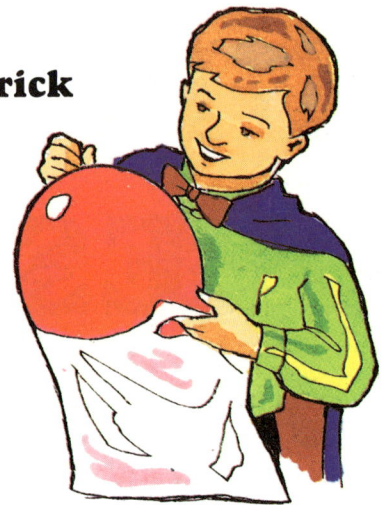

You'll need:

a plastic carrier bag

a pin
2 balloons
(1 red,
1 yellow)

Preparation

Poke the yellow balloon inside the red one, leaving its neck outside. Blow up the yellow balloon and tie its neck. Then blow into the the red one leaving 1cm space between the balloons. Tie the neck of the red balloon.

The Trick

1 Show your audience the double balloon pointing out that it is a red one. Pop it into your carrier bag. Poke the pin through the bag carefully until it bursts the red balloon only.

2 Remove the yellow balloon saying, 'That's strange - the balloon is still there and it has changed colour as well!'

Magician's Helper

To make it easier to inflate balloons, warm them in your hands and stretch them a few times.

MIND POWER

Showing a fork or spoon, you gently stroke it with one finger. It bends or breaks.

1 Hold the fork firmly by its tangs.

You'll need:

an old fork or spoon (get an adult's permission to use this!)

Preparation
Bend the spoon/fork backwards several times until the metal weakens.

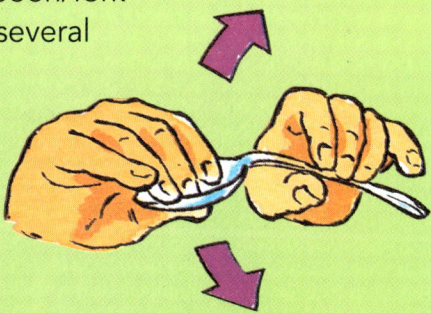

Straighten it so it looks normal.

2 Gently run your finger along the handle several times. As your finger nears the end of the handle, use more pressure. Due to the prior weakening of the metal the fork will either bend or break completely in two.

Magician's Helper
You must give the impression that the power of your mind is causing the fork to bend. Stare at it. Tell your audience about Uri Geller who could bend metal by the power of thought.

27

WINNING BET

Showing a pack of playing cards, you ask someone to choose one. Stating that you can easily find their card, you apparently fail. Your helper bets that you can't discover their card. To their surprise you succeed.

You'll need:
a pack of playing cards

The Trick

1 Ask your helper to mix the cards first. Taking the pack from them, you spread them in a fan shape and ask them to take any card they wish.

2 'I'll turn my back,' you say, 'whilst you show everyone your card.' As they do this, you glance at the bottom card of the pack and remember it. This is your 'key' card.

3 Face your audience again and request that your helper place their card face down on top of the pack. You cut the cards and square them up.

4 Place the cards, one at a time, face up on the table. When you reach your key card, you know that the chosen card is next. However, don't reveal it yet. Deal a few more cards. Everyone will think that you have missed it.

5 Announce that the next card you touch will be the selected one. 'In fact, I'll bet the next card I touch will be yours,' you state.

6 Someone will take up your bet. Pause. Then pick up their card from the table. 'I said the next card I <u>touch</u>, not the next one in the pack,' you explain.

Magician's Helper
When a card is selected, always ask your helper to remember it. Some people do forget - which could be quite embarrassing!

MAN IN THE MOON

A line drawing of a sun is placed in an envelope. When removed, it has been mysteriously coloured in. Everyone thinks they know how the trick is done, but they are fooled.

You'll need:

2 envelopes

thin card

paints

Preparation

Cut the complete address side from one envelope and discard the rest.
This is the divider.

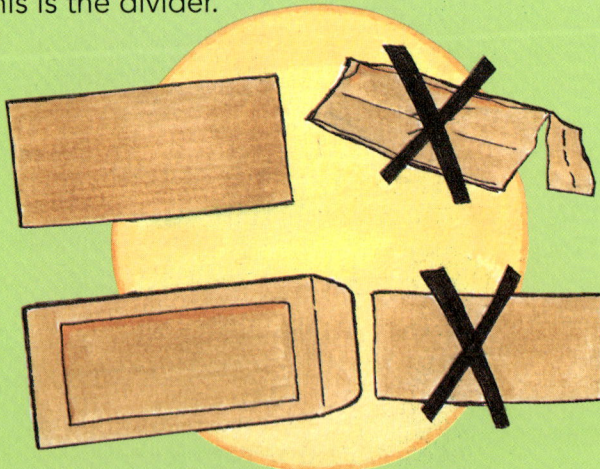

Cut a large rectangle from the other envelope and discard the <u>rectangle</u>. This envelope now has a window.

Slide the divider into the window envelope.
It now has a secret compartment.
Draw the sun on two pieces of card.
Colour one of them.

Draw the moon on a third piece of card.
Put the moon picture, back out,
in the window side of the envelope.
The coloured sun is in the secret compartment.

The Trick

1 Show your audience the black and white line drawing of the sun. With the window side of the envelope facing you, slide the sun picture into the secret compartment.

2 Say a spell and remove the coloured sun. Your audience will accuse you of having two pictures in the envelope.

3 Turn the window side towards them and say, 'You're quite right ..... but this is the man in the moon!' Show them the picture.

Magician's Helper
Trim 2mm from the long side of the divider. It makes it easier to slide into your envelope.

PENETRATING MATCH

You can fool yourself with this incredible trick! A safety pin is pushed through the centre of a headless match and fastened. The match appears to pass through the arm of your pin.

You'll need:

1 safety match

1 safety pin (5cm long)

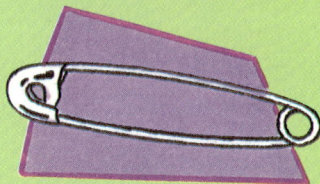

Preparation

Ask an adult to cut the head off the match. Carefully push the pin through the centre of your match. Close the match.

The Trick

1 Hold the pin tightly with your left first finger and thumb. The top half of the match rests underneath the arm of the pin.

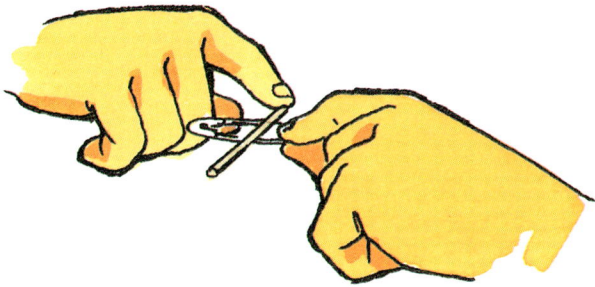

2 Place the tip of your right first fingernail on the end of the match nearest you.
Press down firmly.

3 Gradually move your fingernail away from the match, pressing firmly all the time. As your nail clears the match, the latter will rebound back and appear to have passed through the pin. What happens is that the match ends change places but it happens too fast for the eye to see it.

HOUDINI ESCAPES AGAIN

A helper is tied with two ropes. In a flash, they escape.

You'll need:

2 ropes (each 3m)

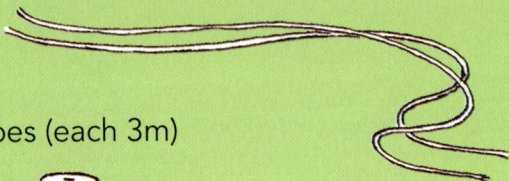

thin cotton (the same colour as the ropes)

Preparation
Place the ropes together in a line. Tie a small piece of cotton once around the centre of both ropes.

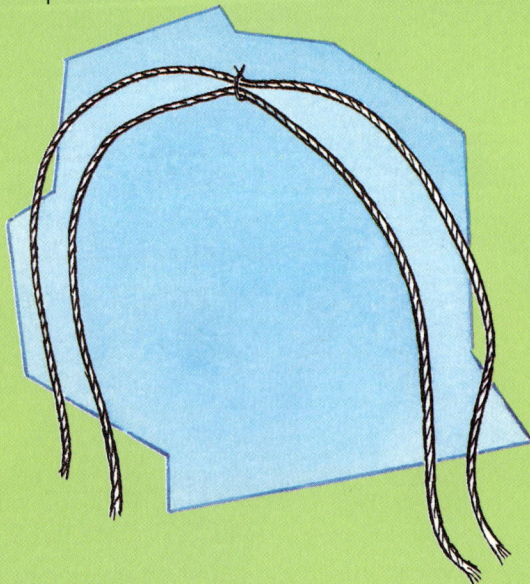

The Trick

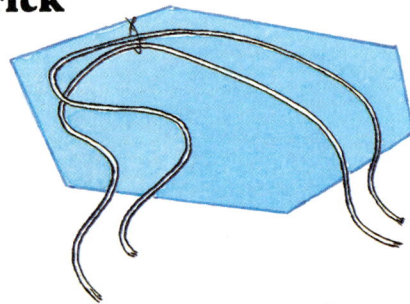

1 Ask two people to help you. Ask one to hold ends A B and the other to hold ends C D.

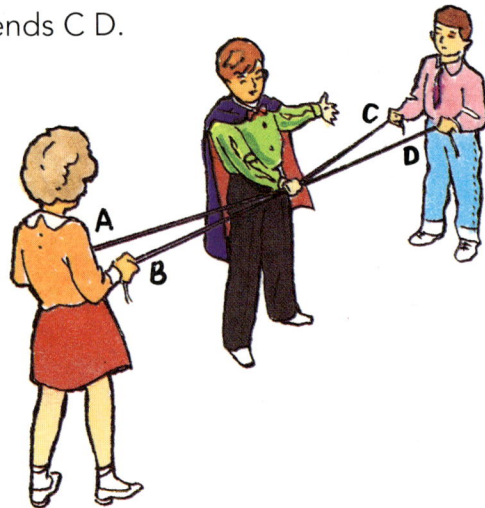

2 'Please pull the ends of the ropes,' you say , 'to make sure they are strong.'

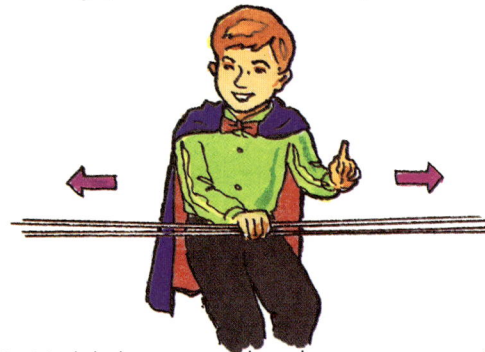

3 Hold the ropes by the centre and request that your helpers let go of their ends.

4 'You know all about Houdini,' you continue, 'he could escape from anything.'

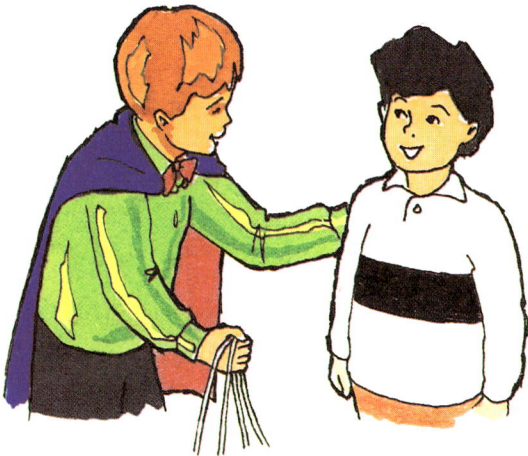

5 Choose a third volunteer. 'You are Houdini,' you tell him.

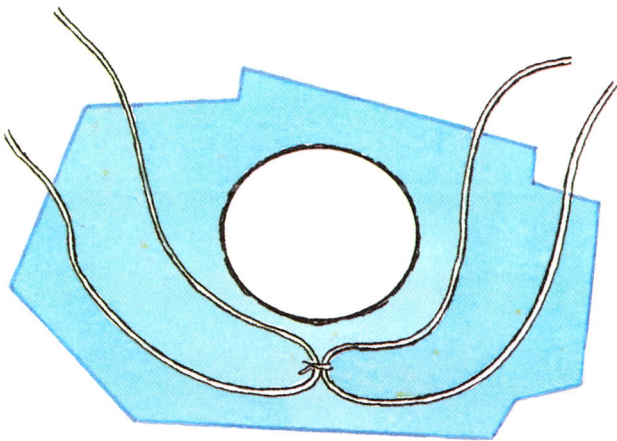

6 Take the ropes behind his back. Bring ends A C around one way, and B D around the other so that they are in front of Houdini.

7 Give A C to one helper and C D to the other. Ask each of them to give you one end of their ropes. Tie these ends in a knot and give the ends back to your helpers.

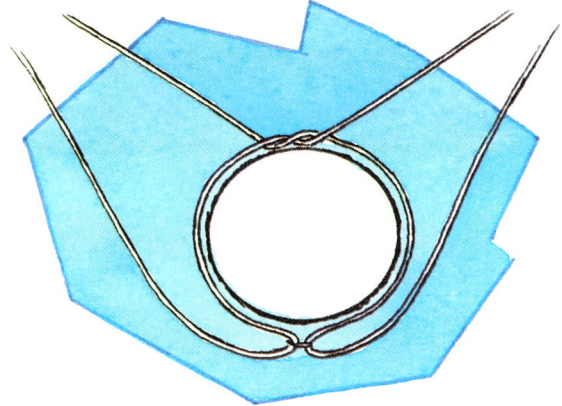

8 Note that the helpers stand slightly in front of Houdini. This prevents them spotting how the ropes are arranged.

9 'Houdini was a slippery customer,' you continue, 'He would escape in seconds. Helpers, please pull hard on the ropes.' Houdini is released. Ask your audience to give him a round of applause.

Magician's Helper
Choose a mending cotton which is easy to break with one sharp tug.

WHAT'S THE TIME, MR. WOLF?

Whilst you are out of the room, someone sets a watch to any hour. It is covered with a cup. On your return you reveal the selected hour. You apparently read their mind!

You'll need:

a cup

a watch (from audience, can't be digital)

Preparation

You need a partner for this one - someone you can trust not to give the game away!

The Trick

1 Your partner notes the hour set on the watch.

(Don't set twelve in the centre far edge of the table - that would be too obvious.)

3 The trick can be repeated two or three times.

2 When he/she covers the watch with a cup, they arrange its handle position to indicate the hour. You've both already agreed that, say, the far left corner of the table is 12 o'clock.

12 o'clock

Magician's Helper

Make a card cylinder (or use a section of a postal tube). Hold it to your eye and peer at the bottom of the cup. This is to throw people off the scent. Someone is bound to examine the tube!

Remember to act as if your partner has no knowledge of the trick and is simply an innocent member of the audience. Or you can pretend that, between you, you have great telepathic skills and he/she is giving you the information through power of the mind. Look at each other and try not to look too much at the cup itself.

DISAPPEARING COIN

Placing a small coin on the palm of your hand, you close it into a fist. On opening your hand, the coin has gone.

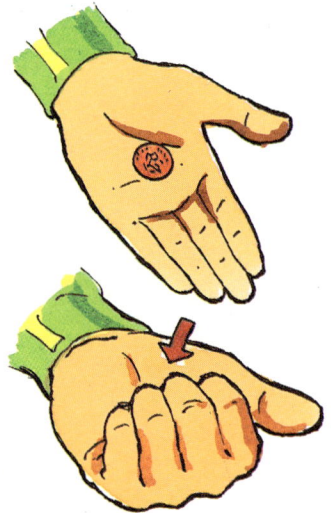

1 Place the coin so that when you close your hand, your middle fingernail presses on it.

You'll need:

a coin

some Blu-tack (or similar)

Preparation
Fix a blob of Blu-tack on your middle fingernail.

2 Open your hand quickly, keeping your fingers together.

Magician's Helper
To misdirect your audience, wave your magic wand over your hand as you open it. Their eyes will follow the wand and won't catch a glimpse of your coin. Remove the coin secretly as you go to perform your next trick.

SLIPPERY BANGLES

A few bangles and a piece of string are examined. One bangle is tied to the string and the others threaded on top of it. Under cover of a handkerchief, you release all the bangles above the tied one whilst a helper holds the ends of the string.

You'll need:

1m piece of string

6 bangles

1 handkerchief

The Trick

1 Fold your string in half. Put the folded part through one bangle and thread the ends through the loop. Pull tight.

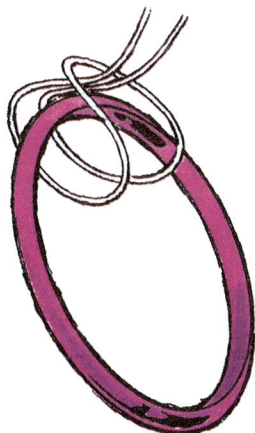

2 Thread all of the other bangles on the string so they rest on the tied one.

3 Ask someone to hold the ends of your string.

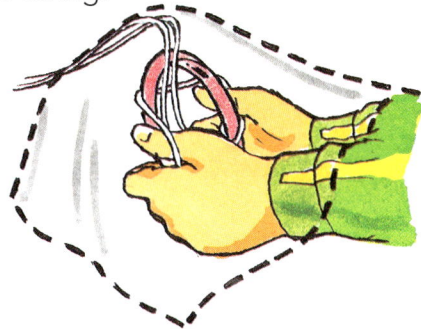

4 Cover the bangles with your handkerchief. With your hands under the handkerchief, pull the end of the loop down and over the bottom bangle.

5 Remove it and the other bangles and replace the bottom bangle. This is done by placing it against the loop, spreading the loop outwards and passing it over the bangle. Pull tight as before.

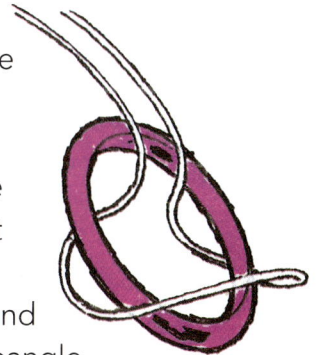

Magician's Helper
You could use curtain rings instead of bangles.

STRAWBERRY AND VANILLA

Several members of your audience are given slips of paper and pencils.
They are requested to write down ice cream flavours: strawberry, vanilla, chocolate, lime, orange, lemon and coconut. All the papers are folded and put into a box. They are mixed up . A helper hands you the papers, one at a time. 'I can always find strawberry and vanilla,' you tell them, 'because they are my favourite flavours.'
You do so without unfolding the papers.

You'll need:

a pencil

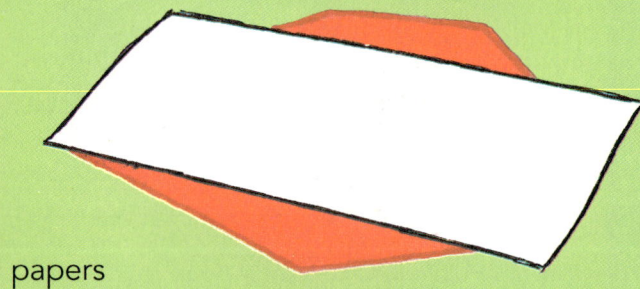

papers

a cardboard box

Preparation

Tear a sheet of paper into seven strips. The end strips will have one straight edge, the other strips have both edges ragged. The end strips are on top of the pile of papers.

The Trick

1 Give your first helper a pencil and one of the top papers. Ask them to write STRAWBERRY on it.

2 The second person is given the next straight-edged paper and asked to write VANILLA on it.

3 The remainder are similarly dealt with - each one with a different flavour on it.

4 Taking a paper from someone, you show them how to fold it - placing each short edge together.

5 Pop them into a box and tell someone to mix them up.

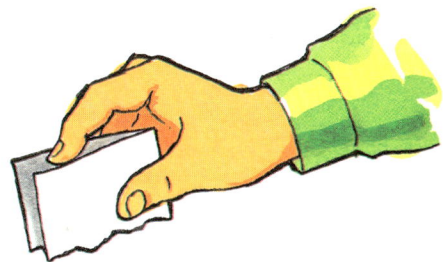

6 You can tell your favourite flavours by feeling the edges - the strawberry and vanilla ones have one torn edge. All others have two torn edges.

Magician's Helper
It adds to the mystery if you hold the papers behind your back.

SECRET SERVICE

From a pack of playing cards four kings are shown. One is put on top of the pack, one on the bottom, two in the centre. When the cards are cut, all the kings are found together in the centre of the pack.

You'll need:
a pack of playing cards

Preparation
Remove the four kings and two other cards.
Hold them in a fan shape with the two indifferent cards hidden behind the second king.

The Trick

1 'These kings are our top secret agents,' you tell everyone. 'Their mission is to steal microfilm from the enemy.'

2 Indicating the rest of the pack, you announce, 'This is the house where the microfilm was hidden. Our spies gained entry from the roof.' Square up the cards you hold and place them on top of the pack.

3 'One of our agents went into the basement,' you continue. Remove the top card, a king, show it casually and place it on the bottom of the pack.

4 'Two of our men searched the interior floors,' you say. Put these next cards into the pack at different places. Don't show these cards, of course!

5 'The last secret agent searched the top floor,' you go on. Show this card and replace it on top of the pack. 'They found the microfilm, but an alarm sounded. Guards swarmed all over the place. But our agents were quick. They all met in the middle of the building.' Spread the cards, face up, on the table and show the kings. 'They made their way to the roof and escaped by helicopter.'

Magician's Helper
Leave the cards for your audience to examine. When they discover that they are genuine, you'll leave them baffled!

43

TAKE A CHANCE

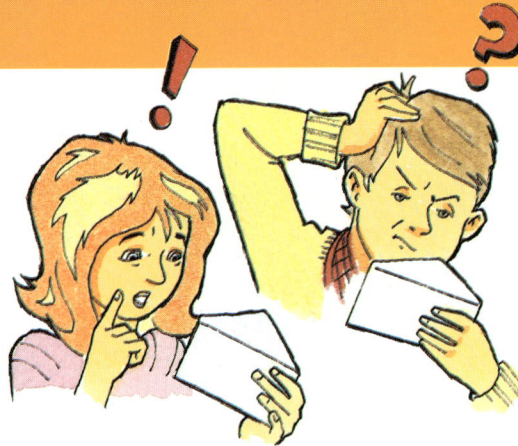

Three envelopes are on a tray. One contains a banknote. Two spectators choose an envelope.
You are always the lucky one with the one containing the money! (Always).

You'll need:

a banknote

three envelopes

a fake tray

Preparation

Make your tray from three pieces of thick card. The centre section has a piece cut out to form a secret compartment. The bottom part has a semi-circle cut out.

The cut out is large enough to take a banknote folded three times.

Slip the note in beforehand. Tuck in the flaps of three envelopes and put them on the tray.

The Trick

1 Tell your audience that one envelope has a banknote in it. Announce that you're 'feeling generous'. 'I will give you a chance to win the banknote'.

2 Let two spectators take an envelope each. Slide the remaining envelope over to the 'loaded' edge of your tray. Your thumb is on top of the envelope, your fingers underneath the tray covering the banknote. Ask your helpers to look inside their envelopes.

3 As they do this, pull the envelope and banknote from the tray. The note is hidden behind the envelope.

4 Discard the tray. Turn the envelope to face your audience - your thumb holds the note against the envelope.

5 Slide the fingers of your other hand inside the envelope. Pull them up and slide the note up until you can grip it with your fingers. It appears that the note came from inside your envelope.

Magician's Helper
Put 'hard luck' messages in the envelopes. You don't show your one, of course!

MUSIC, MUSIC, MUSIC

Some of your audience are asked to write their favourite song title on a piece of paper. You write a prediction. You pick the paper that matches your prediction.

You'll need:

paper

a small button

pencils

a box

The Trick

1 Distribute a dozen pieces of paper and pencils amongst your spectators. Ask them to write the title of their favourite piece of music.

2 Put the paper on top of your button. Tell them, 'I'd like you all to fold your papers four times - like this...' Fold your paper and demonstrate.

> I SHALL OPEN THE PAPER WITH

3 Write on your prediction paper: I SHALL OPEN THE PAPER WITH (title of music) ON IT. Fold this and give it to someone to hold.

4 Ask someone to collect the papers and put them in the box, together with your one. All you do is feel for the button.

5 Hold the paper to your forehead as if trying to divine its contents.

6 When you unfold the paper, slide the button into your palm.

7 Read out the tune title. Then ask your helper to read out your prediction.

Magician's Helper

If you know the tune try singing or humming it.

MAGNETIC WAND

This trick fools those who know the well-known way to do it! A magical wand clings to your fingers. You show how it's done. Then the wand apparently clings to you by real magic!

You'll need:

your magic wand

a panel pin
(a very thin nail)

Preparation

Hammer a panel pin into the centre of your wand. It should project approximately 1cm.

Paint it black to match the centre of your wand.

The Trick

1 When you first demonstrate the trick, the wand is kept in place by your right forefinger. Place the wand at the base of your left fingers, the back of your hand facing the audience. Your right thumb, second, third and little fingers encircle your left wrist.

2 Pretend to hear someone say they know how it's done. Show 'them' they are correct by saying 'You're right - my finger holds it in place.'

3 Repeat the trick a few times, but this time you grip the panel pin between your left first two fingers. Your right hand is in its former position.

4 'If I could magnetise my hands,' you say, 'I could remove this hand altogether.' Remove the right hand and show the wand suspended. 'I bet I'd receive a good round of applause if I could do that!'

Magician's Helper
Use the same wand throughout the show. It allays suspicion that it is faked.